My Heart Sings to the Sea

My Heart Sings to the Sea

POEMS

Silke Stein

Published by

BEACH URCHIN BOOKS

Copyright © Silke Stein, 2023

All rights reserved.

No part of this book may be reproduced in any form without written permission from the author.

Book design, typesetting, and production:
Silke Stein / Maria Ayala

Cover Photo:
Kinga Cichewicz on Unsplash

To those
who find joy, solace, and inspiration
combing shores

Contents

A Special Find 1

Why Mermaids Cry 4

Where Land and Ocean Meet 16

Girls Who Comb the Shore 21

Snail and Limpet 24

Little Sail 29

Bejeweled Beach 32

Seaside Encounter 34

The Sea Glass Sisterhood 39

Present for a Landlocked Friend 49

Beach Butterflies 55

Brotchie Ledge Lady 63

Tide Pool Parties 67

Some Serious Questions for Sea Glass 72

About the Origin of Pearls 78

Our Beachy Afternoons 82

Carapace 87

The Least Desired 89

On Certain Days 95

Sweet Peas by the Sea 102

I've Got the Blues 108

The Perfect Morning 110

Island of the Flowerstones 117

Beach Blessings 129

A Special Find

Is it a wisp of morning mist, congealed

and hardened into perfect shape?

Or, maybe, born of spuming waves

that spread their foam like lace

onto the placid sand?

Or did the moon shrink and drop down

to watch the tides up close

and spend a day of leisure at the beach?

The tiny sphere that nestles in

A Special Find

the kelp blades at my feet,

pale, frosted, softly glowing,

resembles earth's companion.

Or is this gem a mollusk's handiwork

and has, at last, escaped an oyster's jealous care?

But it is larger than a pearl

and not as lustrous and arcane.

Wet by the sea it does reveal its lucid self

and turns into a mini crystal ball

that, if it could, would show one thing:

My Heart Sings to the Sea

An afternoon in late Victorian times,

a laughing girl, dressed in her starched

and ruffled Sunday best,

who runs to chase a flock of gulls,

and, unawares, lets slip

a marble from her little palm,

which has been playing ever since

with shells and pebbles in the surf

until I came to pick it up and take it home

to be its keeper for a while.

Why Mermaids Cry

I like to comb beaches —

it tickles my mind,

the anticipation

of what one may find:

rocks, shells, and marine life,

the tooth of a whale,

some baubles of sea glass,

and maybe a tale.

My Heart Sings to the Sea

I picked up a secret
about mermaids' tears:
There are misconceptions —
the truth, though, endears

those clear, shiny treasures
still closer to me,
as well as the creatures
who cry in the sea.

So, here is the story
of how I found out —
please note that my source was
a credible trout,

Why Mermaids Cry

a steelhead, precisely,
quite large and mature
who just recently had
been fooled by a lure.

It was in the morning,
not past six o'clock;
I walked by a bucket
that stood on a rock.

Its owner was fishing
some ten yards away,
back turned towards me, then
I heard a voice say:

"Please stay for a moment
if you have a heart."
Addressed in such manner,
I could not depart.

In silence, I waited
for things to unfold
and wondered just what
the bucket did hold.

A few steps towards it
revealed a big fish.
The light of the sunrise
served to embellish

Why Mermaids Cry

his silvery tail fins,

which did slightly sway,

reflecting the rainbow

that spanned the small bay.

"I beg you," he whispered

"to grant me my life.

In exchange I will do

my best to contrive

to take you with me on

a visit below,

to the places where kelp

and red algae grow."

My Heart Sings to the Sea

An offer like this one,
you will understand,
could not be refused, so
I stretched out my hand.

The trout in my tote bag,
I ran off, around
the protruding cliff face,
and knelt on the ground

to set my new friend free.
Once in the ocean,
he jumped through the waves in
overjoyed motion.

Why Mermaids Cry

I watched him with gladness
not feeling the need
for further rewards when
he spoke again: "Meet

me here when the day dawns
tomorrow. Will you?"
I nodded, astonished.
"Believe me, I'm true

to what I have promised."
He dived out of sight.
I slowly walked homewards,
and after a night

of little repose, I
returned to the spot —
the fog was just lifting —
unsure about what

would happen to me if
the fish kept his word.
The surf whirled and billowed.
Somewhere screamed a bird.

I stared at the water;
three heads did appear:
a man and two women.
They beckoned. "Come here."

Why Mermaids Cry

Of course, you will ask now

just where I have been,

but I cannot tell you

the wonders I've seen.

I solemnly vowed that

I'll never reveal

if I swam with orcas

or petted a seal,

rode on a swift porpoise

through forests of tall

and swaying seaweed, which

cannot but enthrall,

My Heart Sings to the Sea

or if I met people

whose shimmering tails

had elegant flukes and

small sequin-like scales,

whose laughter could equal

the humpbacks' sweet song,

and if those companions

did take me along

to magical places

I cannot describe,

lit up by fluorescence

and having the vibe

Why Mermaids Cry

of summer night parties
below velvet skies
that host glowing stars and
flitting fireflies.

"And what," you will query,
"became of the trout?"
I'm sorry to say that
you'll never find out

if he was the sea queen's
third cousin-in-law,
the handsomest fellow
that ever I saw.

He took me back after

three full days of bliss

(it's none of your business

if we had a kiss).

There was one more thing, though;

I just had to try

and ask him: "Your women,

do they ever cry?"

He whispered the answer,

his smile broad but coy:

"When mermaids shed tears, it's

always for pure joy."

Where Land and Ocean Meet

What happens in the places

where land and ocean meet,

when sand and pebbles offer

to safely guide your feet,

so that your thoughts can float off

with the receding tide,

and leap from wave to wave top,

or take a lofty ride

on gull wings to an island

quite tranquil and remote

then travel even farther

in a dream-powered boat?

Yet, all the while your eyes scan

the ground that lies ahead

for gifts the sea has left there

in an alluring spread.

It is a transformation

(whom does it not beguile?)

that makes your every fiber

break into a broad smile.

Where Land and Ocean Meet

And any piece you gather

may spark a small idea

that grows into a great one

(it happens often here):

a dainty fan of coral;

a shard of mussel shell;

a perfect spume-white marble

the surf has tumbled well;

some stones with fancy patterns

that are smooth to the touch;

the former homes of limpets,

clams, barnacles, and such.

My Heart Sings to the Sea

All these peculiar treasures
are finds that can elate,
and wake the overwhelming
desire to create.

Whether it is a canvas
painted with deft brush strokes,
a mosaic or collage,
or drawing that evokes

pleasant scenes and memories
of beachy afternoons;
a song that blends the rhythm
of breakers with the tunes

Where Land and Ocean Meet

piped out by merry shore birds;

a charming string of words

with scope and truth and ardor

in all that it asserts;

a sculpture made from driftwood;

a piece of jewelry;

they all will bear the caption:

Inspired by the Sea.

Girls Who Comb the Shore

I am a girl who combs the shore;
it is the place that I adore,
where I will go whenever I
do crave to watch a seagull fly,

and long for salty spray and light,
fresh gales that make my thoughts take flight,
while I drink in the soothing hues
of sky and ocean's gorgeous blues.

Girls Who Comb the Shore

There, any tide may kindly bring
in a surprising sea-born thing.
The surf prepares small gifts for me:
smoothed shards of glass and pottery.

With every treasure that I find,
I leave the weary world behind.
The here and now pleasantly fills
me with such overwhelming thrills.

I dance along the waterline,
and feel true happiness is mine,
while wind and waves accompany
the songs my heart sings to the sea.

My Heart Sings to the Sea

I'm sure that you have felt like this,
have tasted of the coastal bliss,
of sunlit moments at the beach
when perfect peace seems within reach.

So, should we meet each other here,
we'll share the things that we hold dear,
and know we both need little more
than to be girls who comb the shore.

Snail and Limpet

Never before this morning's walk

did ever I reflect

upon a mollusk's life,

what it may think and feel

or do to pass the time.

I might have heard they filter dirt

from water as they feed,

but otherwise I have remained

in utter ignorance about

those ocean dwellers and their creed

My Heart Sings to the Sea

until I found two tiny homes.

For though their owners are long gone,

their shells retain the memories

of days and nights in fluid cool,

of swaying kelp,

and singing whales,

and eloquently tell the tale

of limpet and the turban snail.

The one an easygoing chap

content with a mere hat

of calcium carbonate

(to hunker down below

for shelter or defense),

Snail and Limpet

its top adorned surprisingly

by delicate decors

of pearly gray and hazy blue

and weathered driftwood hues

in elegant geometry.

The other was a tender soul

prone to withdraw into

the secret chambers of

its pointy, winding house

whose sheer perfection would impress

creators of cathedrals.

Where did they learn these skills?

Who drew the plans, made the designs?

My Heart Sings to the Sea

Two creatures barely bigger than
a decent chew of gum
and boasting neither minds nor spines,
how did they craft such marvels?
And there are millions of their kinds,
plus mussels, clams, and barnacles,
all busy in the same pursuits,
the products of their artistry
scattered on shorelines everywhere,
evoking wonder and delight
in random passersby.
Let's cherish and protect a world
where little lumps of flesh

Snail and Limpet

born without hands or eyes

do such amazing things.

Little Sail

I am a Little Sail.

The ocean is my home —

it's where I roam and feed and play.

I have no maps. I make no plans.

Surprises fill my day.

I never know where I will go —

the changing currents mark the trail —

the winds decide the way.

Little Sail

I am a Little Sail,

a jellyfish for sure,

always on tour in company,

with many others of my kind,

devoted to the sea.

Each of us craves to travel waves,

from foaming crest to curving vale,

be it stormward or lee.

I am a Little Sail.

Compared to man o' war or such,

I do look rather shy,

but don't forget to never let

appearances belie.

For if I wish to leap and fly
I'll ask a mischief-loving gale
to fling me far and high.

I am a Little Sail,
and once I even nudged a whale
who was as blue as I.

Bejeweled Beach

Bejeweled beach,

you greet me with a gleam —

your surf all cheer

and spume and gemlike glass.

Bejeweled beach,

my sparkling wonderland —

glorious hours

are waiting to be spent.

My Heart Sings to the Sea

Bejeweled beach,

the thrill of treasures found —

a royal vault

could not bestow such joys.

Bejeweled beach,

we seldom part before

my heart as well

as pocket overflows.

Bejeweled beach,

your beauties are displayed

throughout my home

and in my memories.

Seaside Encounter

At low tide, yesterday, I found

a village on a rock.

The houses were quite small and round,

and white as thickening fog.

"Hello, hello, is someone there?"

I asked the nearest hut,

but not a head rose anywhere,

and all the doors stayed shut.

"None will come out while it is dry.
They are a funny lot,"
exclaimed a crab who crouched nearby.
"Their habits are quite odd."

"If you will follow me I'll show
you some that are submerged.
They spend life upside down, you know."
"Please, lead the way," I urged.

Ten barnacles waved twenty feet
as we approached their pool.
I guessed it was the way they greet,
but Crab called me a fool.

"It's what they do to catch their food,
meals that the current brings.
Oh, look, there are some of their brood —
the tiny, see-through things."

"They swim until they wish to stick
somewhere and build their cone.
A pretty awesome, nifty trick
and skill set, won't you own?"

"I do," one barna-baby said,
and her feet did wiggle.
"Home will be where I glue my head."
Oh, that made me giggle.

"One of my uncles clung unto
a big right whale's left side,
and travelled to Honolulu.
I'd fancy such a ride."

We talked a lot till I returned
to where my bike was parked,
thinking about what I had learned
and what Crab had remarked.

"Don't look to distant galaxies
for creatures that astound.
A dip in any of earth's seas
will proof they do abound."

Seaside Encounters

"They all have purpose — they all thrive.
Isn't that great to see?
So many different forms of life,
so much variety."

While I wholeheartedly embrace
Crab's wise philosophy,
I will refuse to trade my place
with anyone but me.

My head is high — my feet are low,
(none of them adhesive).
They take me where I choose to go,
that's how I like to live.

The Sea Glass Sisterhood

There is a secret sisterhood

of those who love the shore

and stroll along its sandy trails,

eagerly searching for

the jewels that the tides create,

with their persistent waves

those treasures sparkling in the surf,

each of us dearly craves.

The Sea Glass Sisterhood

We share the understanding that
days at the seaside bring,
aware the bond between us all
is strong and shimmering.

At beaches found around the world,
we recognize our kin —
it's not our age, or looks, or size;
we may be plump or thin.

What matters is the way we move,
gaze fastened to the ground,
slowly becoming one with the
sensations that surround

My Heart Sings to the Sea

this place of ever-changing charms,
which prompts us to feel whole
and, even in its wildest moods,
touches our very soul.

Our eyes glint like the glass we hunt,
algae and eelgrass green,
gray as the rocks, brown as the kelp,
blue as the noon-sky sheen.

An ancient impulse drives us on
to gather and collect
what others have regarded trash,
broken, discarded, wrecked.

The Sea Glass Sisterhood

We see the miracle in each

transformed, perfected shard,

perceive the message it contains

can lighten any heart.

The images stored in our minds

are of a certain kind,

the glorious, spectacular

once-in-a-lifetime find:

The vintage marble that did seal

a carbonated drink;

the chunk of well-cooked, frosted teal

without a single chink;

the plain-white bits the sun has kissed,

now lavender and pink;

the multies that seem painted with

brush strokes of brilliant ink —

small accidental works of art;

the bottle stopper stems,

relics of customs long bygone;

and many other gems;

smooth pieces of old pottery,

their porcelain as white

and delicate as the remains

(constructed from calcite)

The Sea Glass Sisterhood

of shells, and stars, and sanddollars,
the coastline puts on show,
those creatures born in salty streams,
sustained by ebb and flow,

which give us glimpses of the realm
that stretches out below
the smooth or roughish surface view,
where few of us may go.

Yet, don't we all from time to time
indulge in daring dreams
of iridescent scales and fins
and underwater schemes,

My Heart Sings to the Sea

in ocean depths, soothing and cool,
of which one seldom hears,
where fish-tailed women spend their lives
and cry their happy tears?

Admit it, you would want to be
a mermaid for a while,
explore the wonders of the blue
that does stun and beguile

us when we stand ashore and watch
the sun's light skip and whirl
in dots of brightness on the sea,
each like a shiny pearl.

The Sea Glass Sisterhood

Whether you walk the waterline

in regions of the north,

rugged, chillblained, and swept by gales,

where nightly skies bring forth

displays of dazzling color flares,

or visit southern coasts,

some tropical scenario

with frilly palms that boasts

turtles and dolphins floating through

clear turquoise lagoons,

and wooden chests in sunken ships

bursting with gold doubloons;

My Heart Sings to the Sea

or if you merrily frequent

a somewhere in between

that is in many seasons quite

remarkably serene;

whether you are an islander,

or dwell at a large lake,

or comb the borders of a whole

big continent to take

away your own quota of joy

and splendid solitude,

and a well-tumbled, marvelous,

glossy and gleamy loot;

The Sea Glass Sisterhood

whether you have to brave the rain,
feet stuck in rubber boots,
or hail July in one of your
becoming bathing suits;

whether you greet me at the beach,
or quietly walk by,
if you love sea glass like I do,
we're sisters, you and I.

Present for a Landlocked Friend

This is the cove I'll send to you
as soon as I locate
a shipping crate sturdy enough,
and watertight, and great.

It is a sweet, secluded spot,
the pebbly beach quite snug,
held by high cliffs on all three sides
in a protective hug.

Present for a Landlocked Friend

Each seasonal variety
of water, coast, and air
has untamed charms, and contributes
much character and flair.

You'll love the misty mornings here
dressed in the hues of pearls,
and the refreshing summer gales
that crest the waves with curls.

There always is a weathered log
of driftwood as a seat
from which to gaze at the blue line
where sky and ocean meet.

My Heart Sings to the Sea

Among the green covering the bluff,
bold flowers greet the eye:
bright orange poppies bloom in May,
pink sweet peas in July.

I know you're fond of treasure hunts —
feel free to shed your socks,
and fill them with well-tumbled glass,
and lovely shells and rocks.

Some critters do not want to leave —
"We live here," they insist —
if curious what to expect,
please check the following list:

Present for a Landlocked Friend

Three temperamental hummingbirds
(fun aerial displays);
a gently bobbing harbor seal
speckled with browns and grays;

A band of jolly sandpipers
(their tunes are never dull);
two rabbits of the timid sort;
one nosy, noisy gull;

One great blue heron seeking food,
quite dignified and still;
a bunch of river otter pups
splashing around at will;

My Heart Sings to the Sea

Nine nimble starfish, purple skinned,
and barnacles galore;
about a dozen spitting clams,
limpets, sea snails and more.

No doubt, you all will get along
together really well —
in so much beauty, space, and light,
everything must excel.

I keenly hope you will enjoy
owning this piece of shore.
Please let me know the moment it
does show up at your door.

PRESENT FOR A LANDLOCKED FRIEND

But if some reason unforeseen

prevents delivery,

I'll send the lines above instead

written for you by me.

Beach Butterflies

Little is known about

those rare, elusive things;

few sightings are confirmed,

and though they may exist

on coasts around the globe,

naturalists did not,

so far, take note, observe,

and classify or name

those curiosities

with fragile, foam-white wings.

Beach Butterflies

So, it is left to me
to tell you what I've learned
about beach butterflies.
Does not the label fit?
I made it up myself.
For it was I who found
the curious creatures first,
on a November morn,
alighted at my shore
after a spell of storm,
nestling in driftwood chips,
perched among rain-washed rocks,
half hidden by the sand.

Why did they choose to land,

right there and on that day?

Frankly, I cannot say,

but sensed that there must be

surprise and mystery

surrounding their affairs.

So, don't ask if it's true

for I believe they do

feed on spume and sunshine

that sparkles on the sea;

and the small sighing sounds

that surf and pebbles utter

resembling a flutter.

Beach Butterflies

They watch the gulls ascend,
and herons, ducks and loons,
and hummingbirds dash by —
"Enough, enough!" you cry.
"All that I won't deny,
but did you see them fly?"
Yes, many times, indeed
(before my inner eye).
They frolic in the fog
of the Pacific north.
They dance above small clouds
that dot a brilliant sky.
They chase the airy spray

My Heart Sings to the Sea

atop a leaping wave,

and catch up all the way

to eagles circling high.

They reach the snowy peaks

of the Olympic range.

Now, do you think that strange?

They trail the sailing boats

that travel through the strait,

off to exciting schemes.

On starry, moonless nights,

they come and congregate

in golden lighthouse beams.

But mostly, I admit,

BEACH BUTTERFLIES

the beach is where they sit

and patiently abide,

awaiting the next tide.

For they are ocean born

and eager to return

to underwater realms

where lush-green eelgrass whirls

and oysters beget pearls,

where schools of silver sweep

through haunts of bull kelp stalks,

where fleshy flowers thrive,

and all the stars take walks

on brightly-coloured arms

My Heart Sings to the Sea

that come in sets of five,
where blue-skinned giants dive
to regions in the deep
full of florescent life.
You know all this is real,
so don't attempt to claim
I told you lots of lies,
for this is how I feel
about beach butterflies.
"But, but," I hear you yell,
"it's just a broken shell!"
Well, well, and so it is,
a simple butter clam,

Beach Butterflies

quite battered by the surf,

the halves still holding hands.

Beg pardon, but I seem

unable not to dream,

or comprehend just why

mundane facts should compel,

or limit what I think.

I recommend you try

and promise you will find:

Imagination lifts

the spirit and the mind,

just as it does propel

my dear beach butterfly.

Brotchie Ledge Lady

Upright and serene,

she does stand in the sea,

for she must be seen:

Brotchie Ledge Lady.

Her gown is spume white

with a broad hem of shells.

Her headdress's bright

and flashing green tells

Brotchie Ledge Lady

all ships far and near:
"This is treacherous ground.
Make sure to keep clear
and sail wide around."

Waves rage and storms blow;
she remains calm and brave.
God only can know
the lives she did save.

Through each starless night
and thick fog breathing brine,
her emerald light
does steadfastly shine.

My Heart Sings to the Sea

Her foot reaches down
to the floor of the bay,
and no-one will drown
if she has her say.

Some mock me, "Come on,
drop this daft fantasy.
It's just a beacon!"
I'll never agree,

but wish that she would
by her presence remind
them of what is good
and caring and kind.

Brotchie Ledge Lady

Brotchie Ledge Lady

may be certain of this:

when she beams at me

I'll throw her a kiss.

Tide Pool Parties

Before a tide pool gathering,

it's difficult to tell

who will be there. Attendees are

invited by the swell.

If the event is a success,

with pleasing atmosphere,

depends upon the time of day

and season of the year.

Tide Pool Parties

An afternoon in June might find
things warm up pretty fast,
while on a February night,
a frosty mood may last.

Allotted are a full six hours —
the moon will check the clock —
and the most likely venue is
a crevice in a rock.

Prepare yourself for random crowds,
complaining is in vain.
Not all are there by their own choice,
they've missed the tidal train.

MY HEART SINGS TO THE SEA

While we enjoy the special guests,
we also have to bear
with all those party animals
who show up everywhere.

For every charming starfish girl,
you usually meet
a bunch of bashful barnacles
who use their feet to eat.

Young mussels will kick up a fuss,
which adds to the hubbub,
and there is always that one clam
who simply won't shut up.

Tide Pool Parties

A crab might drop in for a while
to chat with just a few,
making some legless creatures wish
they could leave early too.

Don't flirt with pert anemones,
remember to stay back
'cause if you schmooze too close to them,
you might become their snack.

If there is space and those inclined,
some dancing may be had.
A jellyfish prefers quadrille —
sand fleas are hopping mad.

My Heart Sings to the Sea

All slugs waltz slow, and algae jive,
and little fins will swing —
this marine jumble might produce
more than one odd pairing.

So, have some fun — the time will pass —
because predictably,
each and all tide pool parties end
with the returning sea.

Some Serious Questions for Sea Glass

These are the things

I'd like to ask

if I could interview

a piece of old,

well-rounded glass:

How has it been

this 'journey' you've gone through,

those years spent in distress?

My Heart Sings to the Sea

You have not started out

like this, have you?

Changes did come

and chips and chinks,

some ruptures too,

that left you hurt,

and some may think

unrecognizable?

Where did you find the strength

to weather and withstand

the high tides and

the winter storms

the constant pull and shove

Some Serious Questions for Sea Glass

of sea and rocky coast?

What did it take?

You must have seen

so many others break.

and being crushed to bits that blend

into a vast expanse of sand.

So, are you glad

I strolled along

to this far corner spot

where you amid

seaweed and pebbles lie,

amazingly serene,

My Heart Sings to the Sea

as if not any wave

moved by the moon

might try

to test your fortitude,

and end

this peaceful interlude?

Will you in years to come,

just now and then,

look back and miss

the roughness of the surf,

the dangers of those days?

Or will you say:

"Not me, I like this place,"

Some Serious Questions for Sea Glass

when you sit on

my windowsill

warmed by a late

September sun

that shines right through

your frosted skin —

making you glow —

and casts a dab

of sheer delight,

as colourful

as it is bright,

onto the ledge,

like a sweet secret, or

your soul, revealed?

Will you then feel

at home, and whole,

and healed?

About the Origin of Pearls

They say a pearl is born of pain.

Can that be true?

Now, when an alien particle

intrudes upon an oyster's peace,

and literally gets

under its skin,

a miracle ensues.

My Heart Sings to the Sea

That is the origin of pearls,

the secret story that unfurls —

the way a small invertebrate

can soothe its hurt

by smothering it

with iridescent loveliness.

What kind of pain

converts to such a feat?

To what does it compare?

An upset stomach? No,

surely not that.

A twisted knee?

A throbbing tooth?

About the Origin of Pearls

While these need care, undoubtedly,

they seem to me

not the sensations to produce

a gem.

What then?

The ringing of a music bone?

That sounds more apt —

a trifle silly, though.

I sense it has to be

an ache that can transcend,

inspire and amend.

Hidden within

this precious sphere,

My Heart Sings to the Sea

this work of art,

I am convinced,

I almost hear

the echo of a broken heart.

Don't you agree?

Only a lovelorn oyster does

indulge in pearly poetry.

Our Beachy Afternoons

I'm sure that you remember

our beachy afternoons,

the ones in mid-September

or at the height of June's

resplendent sapphire brightness

when we walked hand in hand,

carefree and maybe shoeless?

Do you still feel that sand,

My Heart Sings to the Sea

quite soft, and truly seeming
like heaps of sun-warmed gold?
And there were smooth and gleaming
rocks that lazily rolled

in each incoming billow,
which almost reached our feet
with its effervescent flow
as if it tried to greet

us, as we strolled side by side,
so young and so in love.
The sky was clear and so wide,
oh, all that blue above.

Our Beachy Afternoons

We always found a treasure
sea glass, a stone, a shell,
and they still give me pleasure,
and tell our story well,

those small, cherished mementos
of days spent at the coast,
when we first knew we were close,
and what we wanted most.

So many walks did follow.
We faced more than one cloud.
Sometimes we saw a rainbow.
Often, we laughed aloud.

My Heart Sings to the Sea

Later, there were others we

did take with us: a boy,

a little girl. He and she

adored the shore. The joy

of showing them the ocean,

of castles being built,

of seeing them in motion,

their footprints in the silt,

has left such lasting, tender

impressions on my heart.

The gratitude they render,

the meaning they impart.

Our Beachy Afternoons

I can't think of anything
better I ever knew,
except for the great blessing
of sharing them with you.

I've lost count of the starfish
you flung back to the sea,
and if I had just one wish,
it's that I want to be

your one and only beach mate,
forever and a while,
on a late-afternoon date
with your sweet, sunny smile.

Carapace

Who knew crab's clothes are lined

with violet and red,

and pink and purple hues?

We never notice while

their owners live.

Neither do they, I guess,

know what is on their back,

unless they do possess

some strange sensory skills

Carapace

that let them feel

a colour's soft caress,

and make them proud

to add when they are gone

their own small piece

of bright and brilliant,

unexpected beauty

unto the vast

kaleidoscope of life.

The Least Desired

Shared fate:

"I won't stoop down

for white and brown.

They are so commonplace,"

a glass collector said.

"I look for teal,

and lavender,

and red."

The Least Desired

How must they feel
both, brown and white,
weighed and too light,
of no esteem,
zero appeal,
just cruelly snubbed
without a bit
of charity,
thus forced to share
the bottom spot,
last on the scale
of rarity?
I tell you what:

My Heart Sings to the Sea

they do not care,

neither do I.

Their presence does

inspire me

to think and write

words that incline

to sometimes shine.

Here's what I see:

the rich, warm browns

of fertile soil

that brings forth trees,

nurtured by fog,

whose moisture glides

The Least Desired

downwards on smooth

and glossy bark,

in huge, clear drops

as fresh as spume

living on waves,

bubbly and white,

which they have been

a while ago

when they took part

in ebb and flow,

danced to the tune

of tide and moon.

As heaps of white

and foamy spray,

they reached a beach

where woodchips lay

dreaming of groves

with old growth, tall,

so tall their crowns

touch coastal clouds

whose blessings fall

onto the ground

where roots spread out

in fertile soil

of rich, warm browns.

The least desired?

The Least Desired

Not in my view,

I say those two

do hold their own

among the best

and beautiful.

Isn't that true?

On Certain Days

On certain days,

I sit down on a rock

and dip my toes into the sea.

It's at that hour of mystery

when haze half hides the world,

and dew slips from the clouds,

when all is still,

the waves at ease,

On Certain Days

the surf asleep.

and even gulls will hold their peace.

High tide returns,

not in a rush,

but with a gentle touch.

The rising water does caress

the waking land.

I feel its cool

ascending through my calves.

My heels are numb.

Oh, soon they will be one.

I look ahead —

there are some gaps

My Heart Sings to the Sea

now in the fog,

and silver blue shines through.

I long for it to seep into

my skin,

to watch small scales appear

and grow

until they cover what

was once my legs.

And when the misty curtain lifts,

they will reflect

the morning sun

whose pinks and mellow gold

bid me a shimmering

On Certain Days

good-bye.

Then I will glide

off of my stony seat

and float —

the ocean takes control.

Retreating it will carry me

far out to where

wild currents stream,

and dolphins dream.

There I will use

my tail and fluke,

just as they do,

and turn towards

My Heart Sings to the Sea

the waiting deep

that is not blue

but becomes clear

as I submerge.

I breathe in cool

and salty joy

while here and there

owners of fins

watch my descent.

Their sweet, silent

acknowledgement

soon turns into

comradery

On Certain Days

as hosts of friends,

some boasting scales

and others skin,

accompany

me to my new

deep-water home

where I will meet

my longed-for kin.

You look at me

with wondering eyes.

"How do you bear

telling such lies?"

I know it's just

My Heart Sings to the Sea

a fantasy,

a silly and

trite reverie,

imagining

how life would be

for a true-bred

child of the sea,

but pardon me,

on certain days,

I have to shun

reality.

Sweet Peas by the Sea

During three seasons, any plant

nursed by a coastal bluff

may bring forth blossoms manifold,

some gentle, others tough:

the morning glory's mist-white glow,

the poppies' orange buzz,

the Scottish broom's fair yellow bloom,

the thistle's purple fuzz.

My Heart Sings to the Sea

Dog roses, asters, irises,

and some I do not know

will contribute their beauties to

this shoreline garden show.

Yet there is one particular

small flower I adore

whose presence makes me eager to

invent a little lore.

The Sweet Peas' pink abundance charms

the cliffs during the days

when summer's sun illuminates

their petals with its rays.

Sweet Peas by the Sea

Or could it be the mountain wind,

which, chilled by snowy peaks,

is blowing often, who has put

the colour in their cheeks?

Or maybe it is the delight

and genuine joy to be

in such a place with such a view,

close to the untamed sea.

For they are wild themselves, in name,

not bound to any fence

or duty like their servile kin,

chastised by gardeners' hands.

My Heart Sings to the Sea

They share with waves and gales and clouds
this glorious scenery,
and all the pleasures and the thrills
that come with being free.

And yet, there is an odd aside,
I beg you do not scoff,
for every time they cross my path,
I am reminded of

a bunch of ladies, quite demure,
old-fashioned and well-bred,
and each has fastened with a bow
a bonnet on her head.

Sweet Peas by the Sea

They stand together, wonderstruck,
as if they did arrive
from a far land and never saw
the ocean in their life.

Imagine how they, in the dawn's
increasing golden shine,
shed shoes and stockings, and tip-toe
towards the waterline,

and after casting furtive looks,
assured the coast is clear,
undress and rush into the surf,
emitting bursts of cheer.

So can we not, with this in mind,

be certain that the hushed

chit-chats about their morning bath

have left their faces flushed?

I've Got the Blues

I've got the blues

that veil the hills and mountains

with dewy haze

of barely-there azure.

I've got the blues

that sparkle on the water,

twins of the sky's

sapphire radiance.

My Heart Sings to the Sea

I've got the blues

the surf has smoothed and rounded,

and offers to

the keen beachcombing eye.

I've got the blues

that bring a dusky blanket

of indigo,

and kiss the sea goodnight.

I've got the blues

and not one of their many

tints, shades, or hues

has ever made me sad.

The Perfect Morning

This is the perfect morning

to be an otter pup.

The surf is softly yawning,

the sun just getting up,

behind a pastel curtain

of blue and pink and gold,

and all the world is certain,

the rising day will hold

My Heart Sings to the Sea

adventure, fun, and pleasure,
and hours filled with play,
an afternoon of leisure
and naps along the bay.

You are a furry critter
(the cliff face hosts your lair),
the youngest of the litter,
and you will shortly share

a tumble down the rock shore,
and a delicious dive.
What more could someone ask for?
You love to be alive.

The Perfect Morning

This neck of the Pacific
with its grand scenery
makes for a most terrific
personal nursery.

You have a bunch of brothers
and sisters by your side,
and look just like the others:
snub-nosed, plush and bright-eyed.

It's almost mid-September,
and you were born in June,
thirteen weeks to remember,
for fall is coming soon,

My Heart Sings to the Sea

who can be sulky and rude
with oceans pouring down
from clouds in a gloomy mood;
good thing you cannot drown.

When storms will whip the great blue
into a monstrous tide,
large and raging waves ensue,
and you will want to hide.

But now it's time for breakfast,
think juicy mollusk snack,
you always make this meal last
and don't lie on your back

The Perfect Morning

as your kin sea otters do,
who feed floating around,
you have choices, and so you
will feast on solid ground.

While you chew your mussel chops
(the stuff is tasting great),
you gaze at the mountain tops
across the hazy strait

and wonder how a rock swells
to such astounding height,
and if it might be clam shells
that make the peaks so white.

My Heart Sings to the Sea

You hear your tummy grumble,
and know you need more food,
and join the happy jumble
that is your mother's brood.

Drifting along the coastline
in search of yummy fish
with the flavor of fresh brine
that marks your every dish,

you and your siblings hustle,
and plunge and push and dash;
tails, paws and snouts do bustle
in one perpetual splash.

The Perfect Morning

I watch you from the walkway

and wish with all my heart

that I could just for one day

be able to take part

in the funny, rambunctious,

and glorious hubbub

of celebrating life as

a river otter pup.

Island of the Flowerstones

While resting on some driftwood,

I watch an older gent

who slowly walks the shoreline,

a bucket in his hand.

I know what he is doing,

I met him here before;

it is not shell collecting,

removing garbage, nor

Island of the Flowerstones

is he out to find sea glass,
algae, or fishy bones.
It is far more enchanting:
He's picking flowerstones.

They're a rare commodity
and native to this isle.
The tale of their origin
is, no doubt, worth your while.

There was a huge explosion,
rumbling, and lava flow
that fostered their existence
so many years ago.

My Heart Sings to the Sea

And in the cooling rock mass
small feldspar crystals grew,
creating shapes and patterns,
unusual and new.

That is what science tells me,
and who am I to doubt
the theories of experts
who have long thought about

the world and its formation,
and yet you must forgive
my slight dissatisfaction
with their plain narrative.

Island of the Flowerstones

I guess it is my nature
to wish for something more
that has imagination
and wonder at its core.

Just looking at those beauties,
the stunning quality
recalls so many samples
of human artistry:

simplicity and taste of
minimalist design;
a brooch of ivory and
jet, intricate and fine.

My Heart Sings to the Sea

Seed-pearl embroidery on
dusky silk and velvet;
the inlays on a vintage
dark rosewood cabinet;

late-Victorian displays
of flora under glass;
an invaluable antique
Asian black lacquer vase.

Those exquisite flowerstones,
I try to understand,
how was it they developed
without a guiding hand?

Why here of all the places

on the entire globe?

Is there an explanation?

And what are rocks? I'll probe:

They're the stuff we stand on

that holds us up in space;

most of them are hidden

but some rose up to face

us as majestic mountains,

boulders and bluffs, and hills,

whose sojourn is restful and

mostly devoid of thrills.

My Heart Sings to the Sea

They've no legs to carry them,
no branches to spread out,
no shoots and buds to nurture,
no wings to reach a cloud.

There's no sap, nor blood, or growth,
once born they must decay,
and though it's a slow process,
they know no other way.

The ages pass and they remain
Do they ever get bored?
For there is nothing they can
do of their own accord.

Island of the Flowerstones

Of course, there is a fraction

of them that will enjoy

notice and admiration

whenever we employ

them for our needs and pleasures,

to build or decorate,

and many other uses:

palace and paperweight,

some applications lauded,

jewels and marble halls,

and some that are abandoned,

millstones and cannonballs.

My Heart Sings to the Sea

We rip the earth's coat open
to raid her treasure store.
Is she prepared to yield them
or does it leave her sore?

How different the spots are
where pebbles congregate,
caressed by moving waters,
glossy and smooth, and wait

for anyone who fancies
nature's performance art,
in which streams, ocean edges,
and time are taking part.

Island of the Flowerstones

But I should drop my odd and

lengthy ruminations

and re-adjust my focus

(thank you for your patience).

For, have I even answered

the question I did pose?

What about the flowerstones?

Let's look again at those

pieces of dark-grey basalt

and their bright ornaments:

I think they do resemble

a starry firmament,

My Heart Sings to the Sea

or one of celebration

when missiles, shot sky high,

erupt in sparkling blossoms.

I know the reason why!

It is the ever birthing,

bustling, and blooming life

in this special location

that makes things want to thrive,

and has touched with its power,

so irresistibly,

even the barren matter

to a striking degree:

Island of the Flowerstones

with visions of verdure, which

appear in May and June,

profusions of soft petals

as pale-white as the moon,

sweet-scented clusters spreading

below and overhead,

and lilies, tender lilies,

small, humble, and well-bred,

that deck the springtime meadows

with a delightful gleam.

It has to be this island

that causes stones to dream.

Beach Blessings

A large body of water,

hemmed by a stretch of sand,

in whose welcoming, pleasant

softness, I love to stand

and contemplate the wonders

this special spot affords,

the things we take for granted.

But are they not rewards?

Beach Blessings

The world's magnificence and
its experiences,
the beauties of creation
filtered through our senses:

Whitecaps on sea and mountains
and eyes to take them in
while misty moisture tickles
one's unsuspecting skin.

Keen ears tuned to the music
the gale and waves perform,
long locks that like the blowing
of a mid-April storm.

My Heart Sings to the Sea

Bare feet to pace the shoreline

and savour sand and silt,

and the surfs sparkling water

that's always slightly chilled.

A sense of smell that favours

the zest of tang and brine,

the flavours of the ocean

that are fresh by design.

Deft hands to pick the bounty

the beach is offering

and the small calcite marvels

the generous tides do bring.

Beach Blessings

A voice to praise the beauties
of life and scenery
with words that flow in verses
like currents in the sea.

Smarts enough to understand
just what a gift it is
to be a coastal dweller
partaking of its bliss.

A spirit deeply thankful
and, feeling as it should,
a heart pleased with these blessings,
aware that God is good.

ABOUT THE AUTHOR

Silke Stein is the author of the women's fiction novel *Foam on the Crest of Waves*, a captivating blend of mystery, romance, and mermaid yarn, set at one of the world's most famous glass beaches. She has also written two middle-grade books, and is currently working on turning some of her poems into a series of illustrated gift books. Having been an avid reader since childhood, Silke took the detour of becoming a graphic designer before she discovered her passion for writing.

Silke lives at the south tip of beautiful Vancouver Island with her husband and her ever-growing sea glass collection. Long morning walks at the coast supply her with time for prayer, surf-tumbled gems and shells, photos of the pretty things she can't take home, and ideas for her next writing projects.

Find out more about Silke and her books at
silkestein.jimdo.com

Acknowledgments

A huge thank you to Maria Ayala without whose kindness and InDesign skills this book would not have been possible.

Many thanks to my proofreaders:
Debbie Shields,
janet pilewski,
Kathy Allen,
Jill Corley

For more information about
Beach Urchin Books
please visit:
www.beachurchinbooks.ca